THE GRUMPY GRAMMARIAN'S GUIDE TO COPY EDITING

**Active Voice
Awkward Encounters
And The Oxford Comma**

Copyright

Copyright © 2018 by Autumn Tompkins

All rights reserved. This book or any portion thereof may not be reproduced or used in any manner whatsoever without the express written permission of the publisher except for the use of brief quotations in a book review.

Printed in the United States of America

First Printing, 2018

ISBN-978-1-7326157-1-7

Autumn Tompkins

Conklin, New York

www.grumpygrammarian.com

This book is dedicated to anyone who loves to play with words — amateurs or otherwise.

Table of Contents

Introduction 7

WAY #1: LACK OF SYMBOLS 14

WAY #2: UNCONTROLLABLE BULLET POINTS 16

WAY #3: VAGUE NOUNS 18

WAY #4: LACK OF THE ELLIPSIS 20

WAY #5: LACK OF PROOFREADING 22

WAY #6: EXTRA WORDS THAT HAVE THE SAME MEANING 24

WAY #7: WHEN YOU PAD YOUR COPY 26

WAY #8: USING 2 WORDS (TO CONVEY THE SAME MEANING) WHEN YOU ONLY NEED 1 28

WAY #9: LACK OF POSITIVE LANGUAGE 30

WAY #10: 50-CENT WORDS 32

WAY #11: LACK OF CONTRACTIONS 34

WAY #12: WHEN YOU USE THE PHRASE "IN ORDER TO" 36

WAY #13: WHEN YOU USE THE WORDS "START TO" 38

WAY #14: WHEN YOU USE THE WORD "THING" 40

WAY #15: WHEN YOU REFER TO PEOPLE AS "THAT" 42

WAY #16: "THERE IS" AND "THERE ARE" 44

WAY #17: WHEN YOU USE THE WORD "OVER" (COMBINED WITH AN AMOUNT) 46

WAY #18: LACK OF STRUNG-TOGETHER-WORDS 48

WAY #19: "ING" WORDS 50

WAY #20: THE PHRASE "THE _____ OF"	52
WAY #21: CLICHES	54
WAY #22: LACK OF SHORT SENTENCES	56
WAY #23: LACK OF CONJUNCTIONS	58
WAY #24: OWL WORDS (WHO)	60
WAY #25: UNNECESSARY PLEASANTRIES	62
WAY #26: LACK OF THE OXFORD COMMA	64
WAY #27: SEMICOLONS	66
WAY #28: LACK OF PARENTHESES	68
WAY #29: EXCLAMATION MARKS	70
WAY #30: LACK OF YOU	72
WAY #31: LACK OF FIGURES	74
WAY #32: BOTOX WORDS	76
WAY #33: NEW & IMPROVED MUMBO JUMBO	78
WAY #34: BY PHRASES	80
WAY #35: THE WORD "GOT"	82
WAY #36: THE WORD "STUFF"	84
WAY #37: EST WORDS	86
WAY #38: THE WORD "WHICH"	88
WAY #39: FUTURE TENSE	90
WAY #40: PASSIVE VOICE	92
WAY #41: LACK OF (TIME) CONSISTENCY	94
WAY #42: THE EM DASH	98
WAY #43: LACK OF THE EN DASH	100

WAY #44: VALLEY GIRL WORDS 102

WAY #45: WHEN YOU USE THE PHRASE "THE MOST___" 104

WAY #46: LACK OF PUNS...106

WAY #47: LACK OF STRIKETHROUGHS..108

WAY #48: UNNECESSARY USE OF "THAT" 110

WAY #49: LACK OF COMMITMENT TO CURSING - PSEUDO CURSE WORDS 112

BONUS SECTION 114

FINAL NOTES ON SEMICOLONS & COLONS 120

Outro 122

Introduction

This one time ~~at band camp~~, I was at the grocery store picking up ingredients to make ham and broccoli quiche.

As I rolled down the frozen food section too early in the morning to actually care what I was having for dinner, I noticed a woman. She was shouting at a man — upset because she couldn't find frozen pre-cut peppers to make soup.

I hesitated to go down that aisle. But this is New York. And we don't run away from awkward situations. We rush in, avoid eye contact, and grab what we need like a hot, sloppy one night stand.

She noticed me (and my service dog), and her attitude changed. Faster than green leaves in October.

She squealed with delight about my "cute dog" as she walked up to me. And promptly threw her arms around me like she was my BFF from high school.

That's when I noticed the smell on her breath—booze.

I smiled and asked her how her day was. Because this is New York. And we don't run away from awkward situations. (We embrace them like bad habits and diesel fuel.)

She mumbled for me to wait and took off around the corner. I frantically searched for the ingredient I needed and dashed to the checkout. Because this is New York. And we don't run away from awkward situations. But we have our limits.

The woman caught up with me in the "10 items or less" lane. She had doggie ice cream in her hand. She carefully opened the lid and presented it to my dog.

(At this point, I would normally refuse. Service dogs aren't supposed to eat while they're working.)

Instead, I thanked her (I can only imagine how sad and lonely her life must be that she was wasted before 10 a.m.) and nodded to my dog, who happily licked the container clean.

She put the empty container in her grocery bag, planted a big, wet kiss on my cheek, and stumbled away.

An inebriated stranger. With unsolicited affection. In the grocery store.

No, this isn't some x-rated game of Clue.

Only I can get kissed by a drunk while searching for chopped broccoli.

I'm. Just. That. Approachable.

You need your copy to be that approachable, too.

I'm Autumn Tompkins - The Grumpy Grammarian.

As The Grumpy Grammarian, I promise not to judge you because of bad grammar.

Sure, there are grammar rules. But… They aren't The 10 Commandments. And you won't go to Hell for breaking those pedantic rules. (But, in the event you do end up in Dante's Inferno for using The Oxford Comma, I take full responsibility.)

I prefer to think of grammar rules more like speed limit signs. That is — a set of responsible suggestions meant to be broken so that your copy attracts avid readers, raving fans, and loyal customers. My job here is to help you learn how to make that happen

And that means I've got a few new rules. Let's call them a manifesto…

1. Copy editing isn't about memorizing grammar rules. It's about learning how to write faster, better, stronger copy.

2. Grammar, spelling, and punctuation do not define editing. They're only part of the process.

3. Language is a living tool that evolves — stodgy old grammar rules need to evolve with it.

4. Using examples and repetition make learning copy editing fun, fast, and easy. And it makes your copy editing & grammar skills intuitive & instinctual.

5. You don't have to be a great writer to create engaging copy. You just need to know how to copy edit.

6. Copy editing is a skill that anyone can learn.

But nobody's just born with a cool moniker like The Grumpy Grammarian.

It's a title I earned.

During my childhood, there were no…

Magical possibilities of wonder like…Do goldfish bounce? At what temperature do you bake a mud pie? And if you get "fired" does that mean someone lights your pants on fire? Or is that just for lying?

Playful beliefs that you're invincible. And tooth decay is a myth: yes, you CAN overindulge on candy without consequences.

Blissful thoughts that life can't possibly get any better because pizza is shaped like the food pyramid, so it's the only food you need.

Instead, it was…

Tourniquets. Tubes. Tests.

You see, I have muscular dystrophy and spent the vast majority of my childhood in a hospital suffering from chronic pneumonia. My average hospital stay was 3 months. But my longest? Just shy of 7 months.

And *all of that* made me grumpy (with a capital Grump) because staying in the hospital meant…

- No siblings to play with - because they had to go to school.
- No pets to cuddle with - because they weren't allowed in the hospital.
- No Christmas presents - because my family didn't celebrate until we were all together.
- No fluffy birthday cake - because I couldn't eat anything with a ventilation tube down my throat.
- No warm sunshine on my skin - because I was stuck in a hospital bed.

No, I don't want to eat breakfast. It's 7:45 a.m. Do you honestly think I want pancakes that early in the morning?

No, I don't want to participate in physical therapy. I'm supposed to be healing. Not stretching my hamstrings. Do you think I'm going to run a 5K?

No, I don't want to paint, color, or put glitter on ANYTHING. How do you expect me to take part in enrichment programs with all these tubes attached to my body? Let me watch MTV in peace.

When he sang that song to me, it was the first time I smiled in a hospital. For the first time, I knew it was okay to be a Grump. Hell, it was actually fun. Because I was a Grump who got away with…

- Improvised syringe "squirt gun" fights with the nurses.
- Extra time playing Super Mario Brothers with the hospital's Nintendo.
- M & M poker with older cancer patients.

"Oh, she's just Grumpy today. Let her be." - said every hospital staff member.

Because that's what I am.

A Grump. Grump. Grump. And it's Grump-tastic to be Grumpy. Because…

It means I'm being honest with myself.

I'm not hiding behind a perpetual curtain of positivity. Filled with fake smiles, uninspiring affirmations, and endless gratitude.

I'm not ignoring the bad. I'm embracing it and learning from it.

I'm learning more about myself — how to love myself, how to treat myself, and how to be a better me.

When I'm a better me, you get the best of my abilities…

The strong leader

The critical thinker

The objective problem solver

Being a Grump makes me unapologetically happy. But a Grump does need to focus her Grumpiness…

Which is how, over the years, I learned copy editing. And now I can take word vomit that anyone wrote and spin it into word gold that everyone loves to read.

So I decided to write this book. It shows you how to spot certain words and phrases in your copy and tweak them, so your writing makes sense and connects with your readers **on a deeper, more memorable level.**

And let me be clear — learning copy editing isn't the same as copywriting.

Copywriting courses can teach you to sell, and they teach you tantalizing tactics & formulas to craft…

- Killer headlines
- Powerful calls-to-action
- Unique value propositions

But these courses are missing one critical part of the process — copy editing. The ability to recognize whether what you've written makes sense and whether it connects.

And you know what?

That last part is REALLY important.

Because sometimes — a lot of the time — it's not about how great a writer you are, it's how well you copy edit.

I hope you love learning how to be a better copy editor — learn to love active voice, laugh at my awkward encounters, and use The Oxford Comma. And — once you've finished, implement these tips — they'll help you write faster, better, stronger copy in less time!

And if you'd like to learn more, visit www.grumpygrammarian.com. And sign up for my email list. Each Tuesday I send out a fresh copy edit tip.

Grump-tastically Yours,

Autumn Tompkins, The Grumpy Grammarian.

WAY #1: LACK OF SYMBOLS

This makes me grumpy…

When my hyperactive 7-year-old niece wants a latte.

You see my niece likes the same things I do. Dogs. Card games. Sarcastic remarks. Lattes are our favorite beverage. But she's hyperactive, so giving her espresso (on top of her nonstop energy) isn't a good idea.

This is why when we go out on a coffee date I have to ask the barista to make her a FAUX latte. (Decaf espresso, milk & caramel-flavored syrup.)

Brilliant, right? But, the barista usually doesn't understand my order the first time…so I have to try and explain it *without* mentioning the decaf part. (If my niece catches on that she's drinking decaf while Auntie Autumn is drinking regular espresso, there's going to be even more trouble.)

You know what else makes me grumpy?

Lack of symbols.

Because when you put in symbols, your copy is way more fun to read.

For example…

YIKES - Do details like colors, design, <u>and</u> fonts got you down?
YES - Do details like colors, design <u>&</u> fonts got you down?

YIKES - Your Casino <u>plus</u> My Copywriting. Let's create word magic.
YES - Your Casino <u>±</u> My Copywriting. Let's create word magic.

YIKES - Enroll today <u>and</u> turn your badassness into money.

YES - Enroll today <u>&</u> turn your badassness into $$$.

YIKES - 100 <u>percent</u> happiness guaranteed or your money back.
YES - 100<u>%</u> happiness guaranteed or your money back.

YIKES - To enter the giveaway, use <u>hashtag</u> inittowinit.
YES - To enter the giveaway, use <u>#</u>inittowinit

Use symbols to grab my attention. Unlike ordering a FAUX latte…that's guaranteed to baffle the barista. (And get me into trouble if my niece finds out. *Shhh! Don't tell her.*)

WAY #2: UNCONTROLLABLE BULLET POINTS

This makes me grumpy...

You know the strand of hair that just won't cooperate? The one that sticks up, Alfalfa-style. The one that your hair product holds in place like a trophy. The one that even your flat iron can't tame.

No matter how many times I prop my arms up on my vanity & run my saliva-covered fingertips over it...it still won't stay DOWN.

You know what else makes me grumpy?

Grammatically mixed & matched bullet points. (Your bullet points should follow the same grammatical structure. Whether they're past, present, or future tense.)

For example...

YIKES - My services include:

- Copy edits
- Writing text
- To proofread items

YES - My services include:

- Editing copy
- Writing text

- Proofreading text

YIKES - Product benefits include more free time to:

- Spend painting your nails
- Shopping for designer handbags
- Hosted book club with your friends

YES - Product benefits include more free time to:

- Paint your nails
- Shop for designer handbags
- Host book club with your friends

YIKES - Our email marketing system saves you money because we:

- Sent personalized welcome emails
- Automatically follow up with promising leads
- Scheduled 30-minute clarity calls

YES - Our email marketing system saves you money because we automatically:

- Send personalized welcome emails
- Follow up with promising leads
- Schedule 30-minute clarity calls

Grammatically matched bullet points make your message smooth. Unlike that one piece of hair that sticks up Alfalfa-style.

WAY #3: VAGUE NOUNS

This makes me grumpy...

That time when the resident assistant couldn't remember my name. "April...Amber...August..." he stammered. I said..."Autumn isn't a common name. I guess you won't get to scream it later tonight."

You know what else makes me grumpy?

Vague nouns.

So basic. So boring. Entertain me. PLEASE!

For example...

YIKES - April sipped on her soda.
YES - April sipped on her Coke.

YIKES - Amber sketched in her notebook.
YES - Amber sketched in her leather-bound Moleskine journal.

YIKES - August rode her horse to her grandma's house.
YES - August rode Monique, her quarter horse, to her grandma's house.

YIKES - Amy wrote a note to her boyfriend.
YES - Amy wrote a saucy love note to James.

YIKES - Anna hated the taste of those cookies.
YES - Anna hated the taste of those organic, gooey chocolate chip cookies.

To make your copy unforgettable, spice up those nouns. Because obviously, this tip is more memorable than my name.

WAY #4: LACK OF THE ELLIPSIS

This makes me grumpy…

Sunburns and my pasty Irish skin. Do I have a…

Sunkissed glow from a bronzer? *NO. More like Oompa Loompa orange.*

Healthy tan from a day at the beach? *NO. More like boiled-in-a-pot red lobster look.*

Juicy-peach shimmer from 15 minutes in a tanning bed? *NO. More like radiation poisoning pink.*

You know what's more powerful than my hissy fits and the sun's rays?

The ellipsis. It's the most powerful punctuation available to you. It turns babble into sense. It creates drama. And it brings order into chaos.

Use the ellipsis (…) in every piece of copy you write. Why?

First, because it's the best visual indicator for scanners like me …

"You can take a breath here… and here… and here."

And second, because it lures me from line to line…

Pulling me down the page…

…It teases me…

…I follow it until they reach the final punctuation mark.

And, by then, I have actually read your copy.

See what I mean…?

YIKES - We're committed to giving you the confidence you <u>need and deserve</u>.
YES - We're committed to giving you the confidence you need…and deserve.

YIKES - You <u>mean,</u> <u>I</u> didn't send you an invoice? That can't be accurate.
YES - You mean…I didn't send you an invoice? That can't be accurate.

YIKES - If you'd like extra <u>services</u>, <u>I'll</u> adjust our agreement.
YES - If you'd like extra services…I'll adjust our agreement.

Entice me to read all your copy with help from the ellipsis. Unlike burnt pasty Irish skin that won't get me on the cover of Vogue.

WAY #5: LACK OF PROOFREADING

This makes me grumpy…

The winters are so dry in New York, that thanks to my wheelchair, I become a human taser.

Don't believe me? Watch me cruise through my living room, and you'll see the bluish bolt of electricity. Snap! Crackle! Pop!

You know what else makes me grumpy?

Lack of proofreading.

(Please ease my computer-strained eyes & spot every error in your copy.)

Here are 3 tips to proofread your copy like a pro …

1. MAKE YOUR WORDS LOOK DIFFERENT

Change the font type.

Change the font size.

Change the font color.

2. PRINT YOUR COPY OUT

You read differently on a screen vs. on paper, so print a hard copy of your words.

3. READ YOUR COPY BACKWARDS

Your brain automatically corrects the wrong words in your sentences. You become blind to your own writing errors. So read your copy backward to break this pattern.

When you see your copy in a different way, you notice extra errors. (Just be sure to change your font type, size & color back to a professional look before publishing your copy.)

Use these handy tricks to proofread all your copy. That way your errors don't shock me like a bolt of mid-winter static electricity.

WAY #6: EXTRA WORDS THAT HAVE THE SAME MEANING

This makes me grumpy...

I've always believed that if I was going to fail, I'd make it epic.

Winged eyeliner...Sultry? Looked more like I was Batwoman.

Red fedora...Fashion forward? Looked more like I was a starving child from the potato famine.

Green wheelchair...Free-spirited? Looked more like I coordinated with a crocodile.

You know what else makes me grumpy?

When you use extra words that have the same meaning.

For example ...

YIKES - <u>Add an additional</u> $97 to learn how to stand out on a crowded social media platform.
This is bad because add & additional mean the same thing.
YES - <u>For $97 more</u>, you can learn how to stand out on a crowded social media platform.

YIKES - I filled my branding course <u>to capacity.</u>
This is bad because filled means to capacity.
YES - I filled my branding course.

YIKES - Successful entrepreneurs wake up at 6 a.m. <u>in the morning.</u>

This is bad because a.m. & in the morning mean the same thing.
YES - Successful entrepreneurs wake up at <u>6 a.m.</u>

YIKES - My sentences are <u>straightforward and to-the-point.</u>
This is bad because straightforward means to-the-point.
YES - My sentences are <u>straightforward.</u>

YIKES - How to brand your business can be a <u>difficult dilemma.</u>
This is bad because dilemmas are (by definition) difficult.
YES - How to brand your business can be a <u>dilemma.</u>

Make me happy...remove extra words that have the same meaning from your copy. And if you do? I promise I won't make YOU wear the red fedora of shame.

WAY #7: WHEN YOU PAD YOUR COPY

This makes me grumpy...

DIY projects.

Have you ever seen someone with muscular dystrophy try to use a screw gun? I'm more likely to put holes in myself than a piece of wood. Because I want to avoid a trip to the ER, I'll buy a $15 planter from my local home improvement store.

You know what else makes me grumpy?

When you use unnecessary words that soften & pad your copy. Like a push-up bra. But less fun.

For example...

YIKES - He was <u>rather</u> late.
YES - He was <u>late</u>.

YIKES - I never quoted a price to that person. I'm <u>absolutely certain</u> of this.
YES - I never quoted a price to that person. I'm <u>certain</u> of this.

YIKES - The meeting was <u>just around</u> the corner.
YES - The meeting was <u>around</u> the corner.

YIKES - The sale <u>sort of just</u> happened.
YES - The sale <u>just</u> happened.

YIKES - I'm <u>pretty sure</u> the price won't turn customers off.

YES - I'm <u>sure</u> the price won't turn customers off.

Don't pad your copy with unnecessary words. Unlike my DIY planter box...that wouldn't support a single daisy.

WAY #8: USING 2 WORDS (TO CONVEY THE SAME MEANING) WHEN YOU ONLY NEED 1

This makes me grumpy...

That time I was invited to a birthday party and had to get carried up 26 stairs (wheelchair & all) to get there...Only to discover my 4 friends carrying me were DRUNK.

You know what else makes me grumpy?

Using 2 words (to convey the same meaning) when you only need 1.

For example...

YIKES - Sheila <u>spoke softly</u> during her interview.
YES - Sheila <u>whispered</u> during her interview.

YIKES - "My website crashed," Laurie <u>said loudly.</u>
YES - "My website crashed," Laurie <u>shrieked.</u>

YIKES - Anna <u>humorously mentioned</u> her brand's personality.
YES - Anna <u>joked</u> about her brand's personality.

YIKES - Stacey <u>worked hard</u> to finish writing her sales page.
YES - Stacey <u>labored</u> to finish writing her sales page.

YIKES - Harriet <u>quickly ran</u> to get to her client meeting on time.
YES - Harriet <u>sprinted</u> to get to her client meeting on time.

Stop using 2 words (to convey the same meaning) when you only need 1. So your copy doesn't read like it's being carried up 26 stairs by drunk friends.

WAY #9: LACK OF POSITIVE LANGUAGE

This makes me grumpy…

That person in the grocery store, who told me to smile. Dude, I'm going to SNAP at you.

Do you have any idea the emotions I'm trying to eat away? Are you that desperate to see my coffee-stained, buck teeth? Why are you under the delusion that telling me to smile is going to magically change my attitude?

You know what else makes me grumpy?

Your lack of positive language. (Geez! Someone needs to leave an encouraging impression in my mind.)

Unlike that time my art teacher asked me how much longer it was going to take me to finish a 3x3 painting.

Did anyone RUSH Michelangelo while he was creating the Mona Lisa? No.

So why would you rush ME?

For example…

YIKES - Don't get left behind.
YES - Get ahead of the competition.

YIKES - You failed to include constructive criticism.
YES - Please include feedback.

YIKES - Never neglect the details.
YES - Remember the details.

YIKES- I don't have time to offer you guidance.
YES- I'd love to help you. Can we talk next week?

YIKES- You neglected to specify that you needed help.
YES- How may I help you?

I'll happily buy from you when you turn negative language into positive language. Unlike a stranger telling you how to feel while in the grocery store.

WAY #10: 50-CENT WORDS

This makes me grumpy...

When someone makes clicking, gurgling, or smacking sounds with their mouth.

I want to rip my ears off with my bare hands. Which would be quite the sight because I have a hard enough time ripping open an envelope.

You know what else makes me grumpy?

50-cent-words (otherwise known as fancy, schmancy words).

No, shorty. Don't go. It's not your birthday. So save these complex words for your next rap battle.

For example...

YIKES - I got your <u>remuneration</u>.
YES - I got your <u>payment</u>.

YIKES - What entrepreneurial <u>proficiencies</u> do you have?
YES - What entrepreneurial <u>skills</u> do you have?

YIKES - Your copy will be written <u>expeditiously</u>.
YES - Your copy will be written <u>fast</u>.

YIKES - There's a <u>paucity</u> of information and I can't create your logo.
YES - There's a <u>shortage</u> of information and I can't create your logo.

YIKES - I'm a savvy <u>raconteur</u>.
YES - I'm a savvy <u>storyteller</u>.

Remember, you're not trying to impress me or 50 Cent. (We already know all the big words.) You're trying to get us to buy your product or service. Unlike people who make annoying sounds with their mouths. All they need to buy are some manners.

WAY #11: LACK OF CONTRACTIONS

This makes me grumpy...

When slang goes too far. "Bae", for instance, baffles me.

I feel like people decided the word "babe" needed to be updated. But, during the update, the second "b" got dropped. I don't mean dropped in the sense of down a flight of stairs. I mean in a Hooked-On-Phonics-gone-wrong kind of way.

You know what else makes me grumpy?

Lack of contractions in your copy.

You're a human, right? Not a robot?

Then, write like you're having a conversation with me, not R2D2.

For example...

YIKES - "<u>I am</u> heading to the poker game <u>that is</u> close to my house."
YES - "<u>I'm</u> heading to the poker game <u>that's</u> close to my house."

YIKES - <u>Let us</u> design a funky website <u>that will</u> showcase your store's fun knic- knacks.
YES - <u>Let's</u> design a funky website <u>that'll</u> showcase your store's fun knick-knacks.

YIKES - Your <u>payment is</u> late. So <u>I am</u> withholding the final edits until you pay me.

YES - Your <u>payment's</u> late. So <u>I'm</u> withholding the final edits until you pay me.

Use contractions if you want me to read what you wrote. Unlike the word "bae" that needs to be dropped down a flight of stairs...off planet Earth.

WAY #12: WHEN YOU USE THE PHRASE "IN ORDER TO"

This makes me grumpy…

Every time I see my neurologist. And he asks me…"If I take you out of your wheelchair & put you on the floor, will you be able to get up?"

20+ years being asked the same question. 20+ years of the same answer…

"Don't threaten me with a good time."

You know what else makes me grumpy?

When you use the phrase "in order to".

I forbid you to use it. If you do, I'll banish you to copy jail. You won't pass go. You won't collect $200. And you definitely won't earn The Grumpy Grammarian's frowny face of approval.

For example…

YIKES - Stella went to her office <u>in order</u> to update her website.
YES - Stella went to her office to <u>update</u> her website.

YIKES - April left early <u>in order</u> to be on time for her client call.
YES - April left early <u>to be</u> on time for her client call.

YIKES - Harold used exclamation points <u>in order</u> to attract attention in his copy.
YES - Harold used exclamation points to <u>attract</u> attention in his copy.

You don't want me to put you in copy jail. So don't use "in order to" in your copy.

WAY #13: WHEN YOU USE THE WORDS "START TO"

This makes me grumpy…

When I see someone wearing sweatpants in public. It's the ultimate sign of defeat.

Instead of looking comfortable, you look like you just rolled out of bed. Instead of looking carefree, you look like you forgot to do the wash. Instead of looking relaxed, you look like you haven't showered in 3 days.

You know what else makes me grumpy?

When you use the phrase "start to".

(From here on out I want you to picture this lazy verb phrase in sweatpants.)

Like that time I had a job interview. And my personal care assistant showed up wearing sweatpants with HOLES in them. Did she look lazy? YES. Was I embarrassed? YES. Did I get hired? NO. But I did institute a dress code for my assistants.

For example…

YIKES - Stacey <u>started to</u> tell her client why she made changes to her copy.
YES - Stacey <u>told</u> her client why she made changes to her copy.

YIKES - Larry's client list <u>started to</u> grow. Soon he had more than 15 clients on retainer.
YES - Larry's client list <u>grew</u>. Soon he had more than 15 clients on retainer.

YIKES - Anita <u>started to</u> update her services page. She attracted 25% more visitors.

YES - Anita <u>updated</u> her services page. She attracted 25% more visitors.

Get rid of "start to" to entice me to look your copy up & down like a sharp dressed man. Which is more appealing than sweatpants.

WAY #14: WHEN YOU USE THE WORD "THING"

This makes me grumpy…

That time I stopped at Dunkin' Donuts on free donut day but didn't get my free donut. Because I didn't *specify* that I wanted a free donut when I placed my order. Seriously?

Ok, I could've gotten my free donut *if* I'd been willing to go through the drive-thru a second time & ask for a free donut. But c'mon. This isn't NASCAR. I'm not driving in circles around the drive-thru.

Ginger was just as disgusted as I was.

You know what else makes me & Ginger grumpy?

When you use the word "thing".

For the love of glazed donuts, please search your brilliant mind (or your thesaurus) for a more descriptive word. *Don't make me picture you in sweatpants.*

For example…

YIKES - Stan noticed <u>that thing</u> helped him improve his writing.
YES - Stan noticed the <u>thesaurus</u> improved his writing

YIKES - Those <u>things</u> didn't help him be a better entrepreneur.
YES - A <u>bad attitude & failure mindset</u> didn't help him be a better entrepreneur.

YIKES - Sarah told us every<u>thing</u>.
YES - Sarah told us the details of <u>how she balanced her work & life.</u>

I know carbs are brain food. But that doesn't give you permission to act like a donut … drop the word "thing" from your copy.

WAY #15: WHEN YOU REFER TO PEOPLE AS "THAT"

This makes me grumpy…

That time an elderly man asked me why I swear so much.

I mumbled something about it being a form of creativity.

He haphazardly asked me if I kissed my mother with that mouth…

I looked him right in the eyes and told him where I come from that's considered incest & punishable by law.

You know what else makes me grumpy?

When you refer to people as "that" in your copy. Very RUDE. (Sorry. It's actually not that rude. I'm just still thinking about that old man. Who clearly does not prefer The Grumpy Grammarian or her salty language.)

For example …

YIKES - Lance was the guy <u>that</u> charged the most for his services.
YES - Lance was the guy <u>who</u> charged the most for his services.

YIKES - Ashley knew people <u>that</u> wanted help with their branding.
YES - Ashley knew people <u>who</u> wanted help with their branding.

YIKES - Sam rushed to create an ad for people <u>that</u> wanted new graphics for their websites.
YES - Sam rushed to create an ad for people <u>who</u> wanted new graphics for their websites.

When referring to people use "who" in your copy. Don't make me sprinkle salty language all over you. It's simpler than justifying foul language to old men.

WAY #16: "THERE IS" AND "THERE ARE"

This makes me grumpy...

When people trip over my wheelchair.

If one more person does, I'm going to turn purple with frustration.

Purple because my wheelchair is black, so my flashy tee shirts stand out. Purple because my wheelchair is 300 pounds of in-your-face heavy metal. Purple because my wheelchair is less than aerodynamic.

I know you're busy texting your BFF, but honestly...How. Did. You. NOT. See. Me???

You know what else makes me grumpy?

The phrases "there is" & "there are".

These phrases rob your copy of all its power. And dilute your ideas, making me think you'd rather be a big, purple dinosaur than a powerful copywriter.

For example ...

YIKES - <u>There is</u> an error in your copy.
YES - Your copy has an error.

YIKES - <u>There are</u> lots of better, more interesting ways to start sentences.
YES - Start your sentences in a more interesting way.

YIKES - <u>There is</u> no need for you to be lonely in business.

YES - You don't need to feel lonely in business.

Cut "there is" and "there are" from your copy, and I promise not to turn purple on your ass. Unlike tripping over a wheelchair. Because that hurts more than not paying attention while you text your BFF.

WAY #17: WHEN YOU USE THE WORD "OVER" (COMBINED WITH AN AMOUNT)

This makes me grumpy…

That time I bought a pair of white Puma running shoes. And the sales associate asked me (the girl in the wheelchair) if I wanted to protect my shoes from soil & scuff mark damage.

Without missing a beat, I rolled my eyes and replied, "Yes, that'd be great. I'm training for the Boston Marathon & don't want to scuff my new kicks."

You know what else makes me grumpy?

Reading the word "over" (combined with an amount).

When you argue with your man about not wanting his mom to move in with you…you wouldn't say "More than my dead body", would you?

I didn't think so.

Save "over" for when you want to be overly dramatic.

For example…

YIKES - My investment was <u>over</u> my brother's, so he'll make more money than me in the end."
YES - My investment <u>was more</u> than my brother's, so he'll make more money than me in the end.

YIKES - The business coach received <u>over</u> $10 million for her VIP services.
YES - The business coach received <u>more than</u> $10 million for her VIP services.

YIKES - The price of editing services is <u>over</u> $250.
YES - The price of editing services is <u>more than</u> $250.

Stop using "over" when referring to an amount. You don't want me to tell you off in front of your man. Do you? Unlike white Puma sneakers that might get scuffed while riding in a wheelchair.

WAY #18: LACK OF STRUNG-TOGETHER-WORDS

This makes me grumpy…

That time a handsome guy held the door open for me at Barnes & Noble, and I didn't even make a pass at him. (What's wrong with me?)

His kind words & smile lit me up like a Christmas tree. His red hair, freckles, and Carhartt jacket were more vibrant than any Twinings English Breakfast Tea packet.

I should've picked him up like an impulse buy in the checkout line.

You know what else makes me grumpy?

Your lack of Strung-Together-Words.

Strung-Together-Words make my smile shine, like Christmas tree lights. Only without all the pissing & bitching because they're tangled. Or stress-eating 2 dozen Christmas cookies afterward.

For example…

YIKES - The accountant's <u>approach was lazy.</u>
YES - The accountant had a <u>sweep-it-under-the-rug approach</u>.

YIKES - The graphic designer <u>glared at me & made me want to run in the other direction</u>.
YES - The graphic designer gave me that <u>get-out-of-my-way-or-there's-gonna-be-trouble</u> kind of glare. That had me running in the other direction.

YIKES - Even though she hadn't signed a new client in 3 months, my sister still had a <u>great attitude</u>.

YES - She hadn't signed a new client in 3 months. But my sister still had a <u>don't-tell-me-I-can't-do-it-because-I-can attitude</u>.

String your words together to my get my sought-after-attention. Just-like-handsome-red-haired guys-who-hold-the-door-open.

WAY #19: "ING" WORDS

This makes me grumpy...

When non-police people try to give me tickets because I'm speeding in my wheelchair. If I had a dollar for everytime that happened, I'd be rich.

Print-my-own-money-while-living-on-a-private-island rich.

Make-bad-investment-decisions-&-still-be-a-millionaire rich.

Complain-about-the-landscaping-at-my-summer-summer-summer-home rich.

Even though I smile and nod at your "joke", just give me your money instead.

You know what else makes me grumpy?

When you use words that end with "ing" because they add length to your copy.

For example...

YIKES - Mascara <u>was running</u> down her face as she signed the contract.
YES - Mascara <u>ran</u> down her face as she signed the contract.

YIKES - She <u>was learning</u> to write interesting copy every morning.
YES - She <u>learned</u> to write interesting copy every morning.

YIKES - Sandra <u>was working</u> hard to finish writing her sales page.
YES - Sandra <u>worked</u> hard to finish writing her sales page.

You could bribe me to read your copy, or you could cut "ing" words and excite me to read your copy. Choose wisely. I am *The* Grumpy Grammarian after all.

WAY #20: THE PHRASE "THE _____ OF"

This makes me grumpy…

That time me & Ginger went to the county building to pay my taxes.

My wheelchair didn't fit through the metal detector. So…The guard whipped out his metal detector wand & proceeded to wave it over Ginger, but didn't wave it over me.

I laughed and said. "She's not carrying a concealed weapon & a bomb wouldn't fit under her vest." The guard didn't see the humor. And I ended up with an escort to pay my taxes.

You know what else makes me & Ginger grumpy?

The phrase "the _____ of".

I know you want to sound as professional as possible. But you're reducing the potential for your copywriting to impact your readers. *Like a soggy potato chip.*

Cut "the _____ of" to make your copy crisper than a Lay's potato chip.

For example…

YIKES - The state of freelancing is fraught with customers not paying for services.
YES - Freelancing is fraught with customers not paying for services.

YIKES - The field of branding is booming.
YES - Branding is booming.

YIKES - <u>The act of invoicing</u> scares new entrepreneurs.

YES - <u>Invoicing</u> scares new entrepreneurs.

Cut "the _____ of" and make your copy more impactful than an armed guard escort.

WAY #21: CLICHES

This makes me grumpy...

That time I tried to sing my niece a nursery rhyme. But couldn't remember the lyrics.

I sat there remixing Bah Bah Black Sheep & Mary Had A Little Lamb. Like some Beastie Boys' mashup.

And got AGITATED.

About 24-ish years ago, I was given a medication to help me forget the pain caused by spinal fusion surgery.

It wiped my long-term memory.

Because I forgot everything I learned from kindergarten through 3rd grade (and only had 1 year to relearn elementary school), subjects were prioritized.

Math was more important than nursery rhymes.

So instead of singing my niece a nursery rhyme, I sang her the times table.

You know what else makes me grumpy?

Cliches.

These overused expressions lack word originality, word ingenuity, and word impact. They fail to excite, motivate, or impress your readers.

For example...

YIKES - Our services <u>sell like hotcakes</u>.

YES - We're booked 7 months in advance because our services are ooey-gooey-brownie good.

YIKES - Avoid cliches <u>like the plague</u>.
YES - Cut cliches to add excitement to your copy.

YIKES - Stock photos are <u>a dime a dozen</u>.
YES - The same generic stock photos seem to appear on everyone's website.

To add excitement to your copy, get rid of cliches Don't make me erase your memory. It's easier than remembering nursery rhymes.

WAY #22: LACK OF SHORT SENTENCES

This makes me grumpy…

After a long & cold New York winter, I love a roaring bonfire coupled with a strong libation.

The crackle of the wood. The burn of the whiskey. I'm one happy camper.

But facial irritation from the bonfire's flames? No thanks. I burn easily. So Hell really isn't an option for me.

You know what else makes me grumpy?

Reading long sentences.

Short sentences give your copy life. And add energy to it.

Like Red Bull. Short sentences give your words wings.

So keep your sentences 9-11 words.

For example…

YIKES - We are so excited about our new flavor of ice cream that we want to give you a free scoop of it. No, seriously!
YES - We're so excited about our new flavor of ice cream. Here's a free scoop just because. No, seriously!

YIKES - Our Community Credit Union has been called many things over the years including forward-thinking, eco-friendly, and convenient.

YES - Community Credit Union has been called many things over the years. Forward-thinking. Eco-Friendly. Convenient.

YIKES - If you want to join my email list just sign up here and get ready to receive tips every Tuesday.
YES - Sign up here for my email list & receive tips every Tuesday.

To make your copy more engaging & easier to read, cut sentence length. Unlike porcelain skin. Which isn't ideal for bonfires or Hell.

WAY #23: LACK OF CONJUNCTIONS

This makes me grumpy...

Getting a song stuck in my head.

Remember that catchy little line from Schoolhouse Rocks..."Conjunction junction. What's your function?" (Is it stuck in your head now, too?)

My answer to that notorious question: To make your copy more interesting, of course.

Starting sentences with "and", "but", or "or" gives you more control over the tone & flow of your copy. It also adds variety and keeps your sentence short.

So use conjunctions in your copy. Or else you'll hear my voice in your head. And I promise I won't be singing a cutesy Schoolhouse Rocks song.

For example...

YIKES - I hate to waste a drop of gas <u>and drive</u> for miles because it's so expensive.
YES - I hate to waste a drop of gas. <u>And drive</u> for miles because it's so expensive.

YIKES - I wanted to go to the beach, <u>but I</u> had too much client work.
YES - I wanted to go to the beach. <u>But I</u> had too much client work.

YIKES - I don't want to pay for graphic design <u>or web design</u> because I can do it myself.
YES - I don't want to pay for graphic design. <u>Or web design</u> because I can do

it myself.

To entice readers to read more of your copy, use conjunctions. Unlike catchy kids' tunes that get stuck in your head.

WAY #24: OWL WORDS (WHO)

This makes me grumpy…

When someone wishes me (the girl named Autumn) a Happy Fall and/or Happy Equinox. I just smile & drive away. I don't need that kind of negativity in my life.

You know what else makes me grumpy?

When you transform into an owl and refer to an inanimate object (like a business, a store, or an airport) like it's a person. AKA—Owl Words.

A business is made of people, right? Yes. But is a business a person? No.

So when you're talking about a business in your copy, use "its". Not "who" or "their".

(Unless you're British or writing for a British audience. Then, of course, carry on with your use of "who" and "their" for inanimate objects.)

For example...

YIKES - The store, who sells the most slushies, wins a free makeover for their kitchen.
YES - The store that sells the most slushies wins a free makeover for its kitchen.

YIKES - The airport, whose logo is a cloud, has their own fleet of 100 planes.
YES - The airport's logo is a cloud and has its own fleet of 100 planes.

YIKES - The company, who hires freelancers at their discretion, wants you.
YES - The company hires freelancers at its discretion and wants you.

When referring to businesses, use "its", not "who". It makes me happier than the arrival of fall.

WAY #25: UNNECESSARY PLEASANTRIES

This makes me grumpy…

On the list of life-shattering events that horrify me—running into my gynecologist in the grocery store is at the top. And by "running into" I don't mean with my wheelchair. Because that'd be way more fun than what I actually mean…rolling down the drink aisle & locking eyes with her. Exchanging pleasantries as I grab my vanilla flavored coffee syrup. And frantically dash to the checkout.

Because the only thought in my mind is…

You've seen me naked. Let's not pretend we're friends.

You know what else makes me grumpy?

You using words like…

- Welcome
- Please
- Thank you

These are all unnecessary pleasantries in copywriting. Those words don't engage me or your readers. Or entice us to read more of your copy.

Stop being polite. And get to the point of your message.

For example…

YIKES - <u>Welcome</u> to our website. Learn how to build your brand with us.

YES - Learn how to effortlessly build your brand.

YIKES - <u>Please</u> fill out our survey and let us know how we're doing.
YES - Fill out our survey & tell us how we're doing.

YIKES - <u>Thank you</u> for your input. Here's a discount toward your next purchase.
YES - Congratulations...You've earned a discount for your valuable insight.

To get to the point of your message, cut unnecessary pleasantries. It's nicer than an awkward encounter with your gynecologist at the grocery.

WAY #26: LACK OF THE OXFORD COMMA

This makes me grumpy…

Getting a new muffler for my van from the auto-parts store and seeing the sales associate readjusted his man parts. He tried to shake my hand after he carried the car part to my van. I slowly curled my hands and pretended I couldn't.

(Just one of the many daily perks of having a disability.)

You know what else makes me grumpy?

You not using The Oxford Comma.

Think of it as the old fashioned way to write bullet points. Full of clarity and class.

The Oxford Comma is ALWAYS placed before "and" or "or".

It separates items in a list. Without this comma, the items in your list become unintentionally humorous & simultaneously confusing.

Remember, you want me to laugh with you, not at you.

For example…

YIKES - Highlights of my client list include a <u>jeweler, a music producer and a dildo collector</u>.
YES - Highlights of my client list include a <u>jeweler, a music producer, and a dildo collector</u>.

YIKES - I love my <u>parents, Lady Gaga and The Tooth Fairy</u>.
YES - I love my <u>parents, Lady Gaga, and The Tooth Fairy</u>.

YIKES - I dedicate this award to my <u>good friends, Young Jeezy and God.</u>
YES - I dedicate this award to my <u>good friends, Young Jeezy, and God.</u>

To cut confusion from your copy, use the Oxford Comma. Unlike pretending you're more disabled than you actually are.

WAY #27: SEMICOLONS

This makes me grumpy…

Getting catheterized because of chronic UTIs when I was a kid. And slapping the doctor across the face in retaliation.

You know what else makes me grumpy?

Semicolons.

Semicolons connect 2 or more independent clauses to show a closer relationship. It stinks up your copy and confuses me.

Cut semicolons & replace with a dash or period to add clarity to your copy.

For example:

YIKES - I ordered the following <u>supplies; pens</u>, paper, and printer ink.
YES - I ordered the following <u>supplies - pens</u>, paper, and printer ink.

YIKES - Entrepreneurs are <u>noble souls; they have</u> brave hearts.
YES - Entrepreneurs are <u>noble souls. They have</u> brave hearts.

YIKES - Tom edits <u>novels; his friend</u> edits comic books.
YES - Tom edits <u>novels - his friend</u> edits comic books.

To guarantee your copy's success, get rid of semicolons. Unlike a child slapping her doctor. Which guarantees a catheter.

WAY #28: LACK OF PARENTHESES

This makes me grumpy…

That time I wrote my first college essay, got an "F", and confronted TA Ray about it.

He told me I must have a big dick to question his grading policy. I said…Yeah, it barely fit through the door. Didn't you see me struggling to get into the room?

He blushed and changed my grade to a "C".

You know what else makes me grumpy?

Lack of parentheses in your copy.

Parentheses engage your readers. (Stick around & I'll show you.)

It makes them feel like you're sharing a secret (just don't tell anyone…).

And everyone loves secrets. (Don't you?)

For Example…

YIKES - I had a product-development epiphany.
YES - I had a product-development epiphany <u>(while dozing off on the beach)</u>.

YIKES - We headed toward the summit of our product completion.
YES - We headed toward the summit of our product completion <u>(a goal we had anticipated accomplishing all week)</u>.

YIKES - Being a copy editor is a tough job that puts a lot of stress on my shoulders.

YES - Being a copy editor is a tough job that puts a lot of stress on my shoulders <u>(false: I love every second of it)</u>.

To create a compelling message, use parentheses in your copy. Unlike trying to swing a big dick through the door.

WAY #29: EXCLAMATION MARKS

This makes me grumpy…

That time I roll into my local gym…

And pick up a membership application…

For my service dog.

I thought the owner was going to laugh me out of the place after I asked her if she'd let my dog burn off some energy on the treadmill.

All she said was this isn't a dog gym, but what's the worst that could happen?

I said…Hopefully, no one is allergic.

To which she replied…People are allergic to the gym equipment, not dogs.

You know what else makes me grumpy?

Exclamation marks.

Instead of creating excitement, exclamation marks become visual roadblocks. Readers stop reading your copy & try to decipher what's so exciting. Then, you've lost their attention.

Using them is equal to painting eyebrows on the Mona Lisa.

Replace them with other punctuation or capitalization.

For example…

YIKES - The accountant was fast!
YES - The accountant was...fast.

YIKES - Gene actually signed the contract. No way!
YES - Gene actually signed the contract - no way.

YIKES - She signed 3 retainer clients in one day!
YES - She signed 3 retainer clients in ONE day.

To end fake excitement in your copy, get rid of exclamation marks. It creates more interest than a dog with a gym membership.

WAY #30: LACK OF YOU

This makes me grumpy…

That time my neighbor saw me move my legs. And told me I shouldn't become dependant on my wheelchair (like it's a drug habit).

You know what else makes me grumpy?

Lack of the pronoun "you" in your copy.

"You" personalizes your copy & instantly creates engagement.

In this case, the world doesn't revolve around me (unfortunately). It revolves around "you".

For example…

YIKES - We offer a discount to a new customer.
YES - You get a discount because you're a new customer.

YIKES - Our team is dedicated.
YES - You enjoy dedicated services tailored to fit your needs.

YIKES - We love our clients and give them the best.
YES - You're special and deserve to receive the best.

Change every "we" to "you", so your copy feels personal. It's easier than explaining a neuromuscular disease to your neighbor.

WAY #31: LACK OF FIGURES

This makes me grumpy…

That time a horse bit me on the knee because I smelled like corn. Milkshakes might bring all the boys to your yard. But corn smells bring all the horses to mine.

You know what else makes me grumpy?

Lack of figures in your copy.

The grammar rule that says "write out numbers 9 and below & use figures for 10 and above"…

…Doesn't apply to copywriting.

Figures call attention to themselves and make your copy stand out like a bad toupee or a wheelchair.

For example…

YIKES - You get more than <u>two hundred</u> investment secrets to boost your wealth.
YES - You get more than <u>200</u> investment secrets to boost your wealth.

YIKES - The Widget 3000 is only <u>seventy-nine dollars</u> including shipping and tax.
YES - The Widget 3000 is only <u>$79</u> including shipping and tax.

YIKES - There were <u>one hundred fifty</u> people present at the conference.
YES - There were <u>150</u> people present at the conference.

Use figures to call attention to numbers in your copy. Unlike corn that attracts every horse in the stable.

WAY #32: BOTOX WORDS

This makes me grumpy…

Eating a delicious dessert "made with love" by my 7-year-old niece and never knowing if I'm going to get sick.

And just in case you don't know "made with love" includes special ingredients like…

- Hair
- Egg Shells
- Fuzz
- Excessive Sprinkles
- A Surprise Sneeze

(It's a good thing I have a standing order for antibiotics from my doctor.)

You know what else makes me grumpy?

Filler words—AKA Botox Words.

Like Botox, these emotionless words inject with filler words that seem impressive. But aren't. The only thing they do is give me wrinkles.

For example…

YIKES - Our products are market-leading.
YES - Our products change the way you eat.

YIKES - Our cars are best-in-class.

YES - Our cars keep you safe while looking stylish.

YIKES - Our web hosting is world-class.
YES - Our web hosting service guarantees your site will never be down.

YIKES - We provide state-of-the-art editing services.
YES - Our editors take monthly refresher classes to ensure you receive the best services.

YIKES - Our graphic design services use industry-standard software.
YES - Our designers use quality software to provide you with beautiful graphics.

To keep your readers' attention, cut Botox Words. Just like looking for special ingredients in your cupcake.

WAY #33: NEW & IMPROVED MUMBO JUMBO

This makes me grumpy…

That time GQ Magazine interviewed Phil Robertson from Duck Dynasty.

Everyone's like *he's so ruggedly handsome*. And I'm like *that publication is definitely off my lady-boner list of "must read magazines"*.

You know what else makes me grumpy?

Copy filled with NEW & IMPROVED mumbo jumbo.

You didn't invent the wheel. You didn't discover the cure for cancer. You didn't decide this season's shoe trend.

So please, don't inflate your copy with unsubstantiated claims.

For example…

YIKES - Our products are NEW & IMPROVED.
YES - Our app changes the way you do business by automatically tallying all your invoices.

YIKES - Our steampunk hats are NEW & IMPROVED.
YES - Our steampunk hats make you feel like you're the captain of your own ship.

YIKES - Our next-generation editing services are NEW & IMPROVED.
YES - Our editing services ensure your copy converts prospects into paying clients.

Cut NEW & IMPROVED mumbo jumbo from your copy. Unlike aesthetically displeasing men in GQ.

WAY #34: BY PHRASES

This makes me grumpy…

That time I got a new wheelchair, the seat was 2 inches wider than it needed to be, and the company told me it's policy to do that. Because everyone who uses a wheelchair gets fat. Except I've never weighed more than 80 pounds my entire life.

It's all fun & games until you go around a corner, slide in your chair (like it's a bumper car), and break your door.

You know what else makes me grumpy?

"By" phrases.

Instead of your copy feeling like a newspaper boy from the 1920s shouting, "Extra. Extra. Read all about it!" It feels like a superhero gave up.

For example…

YIKES - The invoice was changed <u>by</u> Sue.
YES - Sue changed the invoice.

YIKES - The novel was edited <u>by</u> me in one day.
YES - I edited the novel in one day.

YIKES - A scathing review of my product was written <u>by</u> my client.
YES - My client wrote a scathing review of my product.

Get rid of "by" phrases to make your copy ACTIVE. It's easier than getting called fat.

WAY #35: THE WORD "GOT"

This makes me grumpy...

That time I was scolded for using my name tag as a coaster. For my 100 proof Southern Comfort during a networking event.

That's a no-no. Apparently, it insults the wait staff & no one knows your name.

All I can think is...This isn't the TV show Cheers. Not everybody needs to know my name.

You know what else makes me grumpy?

Using the word "got" in your copy.

Got is a vague word.

While "got" is fine for conversations, it's not an effective copywriting word.

Get rid of this word. Cuz ain't nawbody got tyme fur dat.

For example...

YIKES - Well, she's <u>got</u> something to take her mind off it now.
YES - Client work took her mind off her troubles.

YIKES - When I was 17, I <u>got</u> a Macintosh computer.
YES - When I was 17, I bought my first Macintosh computer.

YIKES - I quickly <u>got</u> into the makeup fun.
YES - I discovered the fun of makeup and jumped into it, lips first.

Cut "got" to make your copy more actionable. Unlike insulting wait staff.

WAY #36: THE WORD "STUFF"

This makes me grumpy…

That time I applied for a heavy-equipment-operator position at a construction company. And didn't get the job.

My power wheelchair weighs 308 pounds (without me sitting in it). Technically, that classifies it as heavy equipment.

The interviewer laughed and ended our session after 5 minutes.

You know what else makes me grumpy?

Using the word "stuff" in your copy.

"Stuff" is a generic word.

While you might know exactly what "stuff" you're talking about, readers might not.

Instead of distracting me with "stuff", distract me with a latte, or a handsome man, or a handsome man holding a latte.

For example...

YIKES - She shuddered as she applied a thin film of the <u>stuff</u> to her lips.
YES - She shuddered as she applied a thin film of the <u>flavorful gloss</u> to her lips.

YIKES - This is important <u>stuff</u> and risky as Hell in business.
YES - <u>Viewpoints are important</u> and risky as Hell in business.

YIKES - My client refused to do <u>stuff</u> like that.

YES - My client refused to pick his logo colors and take part in his rebrand in any way.

Cut "stuff". It's more engaging than getting laughed out of an interview.

WAY #37: EST WORDS

This makes me grumpy…

That time I had an echocardiogram and the technician was a handsome dude. I could tell he was uncomfortable, so I tried to lighten the mood with a joke about taking my clothes off. It eased his apprehension. And I learned too much about his life as drummer & his groupies.

Every time I meet a sweet-looking fella, and I'm always the one taking my clothes off. He never reciprocates.

You know what else makes me grumpy?

Words that end in EST.

"Fastest", "strongest", "bestest"…These words don't tell your readers anything.

For example…

YIKES - We have the fast<u>est</u> sign up ever.
YES - Sign up in 3 steps.

YIKES - We have the strong<u>est</u> website security.
YES - Our security protects 12 million websites from hackers everyday.

YIKES - We have the tasti<u>est</u> burgers in town.
YES - 87% of our customers buy a second burger.

Get rid of words that end in EST. It's easier than taking your clothes off in front of a handsome technician.

WAY #38: THE WORD "WHICH"

This makes me grumpy…

That time I was playing tag with my childhood friends. And lost because the tire on my wheelchair fell off. And I landed on the ground. Nothing says, "you're still a winner," like five 12-year-olds trying to put your wheelchair back in an upright position.

I don't know what bruised more. My ribs or my ego.

You know what else makes me grumpy?

Using the word "which" in your copy.

For example…

YIKES - The copywriting books, <u>which</u> have red covers, are new.
YES - The new copywriting books have red covers.

YIKES - Branding classes, <u>which</u> are held on Wednesdays, are in building 206.
YES - Branding classes are taught on Wednesdays in building 206.

YIKES - Our logo package, <u>which</u> is the most popular, costs $799.
YES - Our high-end logo package for established businesses costs $799.

Stop using WHICH. It's more fun than losing a game of tag because the wheel fell off your wheelchair.

WAY #39: FUTURE TENSE

This makes me grumpy…

That time I was rolling through the Oakdale Mall carrying a reciprocal saw that needed to be repaired.

People were staring at me more than usual. Offended, I assumed it was because of my wheelchair.

Halfway up the elevator, as I ranted about how discrimination is still prevalent in this country, my friend points out that my reciprocal saw could easily be mistaken for a sawed-off shotgun because of the way I was carrying it.

No wonder why they were staring. Apparently, a girl confined to a wheelchair, carrying a power tool, was potential mass-murderer.

You know what else makes me grumpy?

Future tense.

It implies that you've never done anything before, and this is your first time doing it.

Use present simple tense instead. This implies you have an ongoing benefit or point of experience. Present simple tense says not only can you do something, but you are doing it.

For example...

YIKES - I <u>will work</u> with contacts across the globe.
YES - I <u>work</u> with contacts across the globe.

YIKES - Our methods <u>will be successful</u>.
YES - Our methods <u>never fail</u>.

YIKES - He will <u>never forget</u> the services he offers.
YES - He <u>never forgets</u> the services he offers.

Use present simple tense to show action in your copy. It's less offending than a power tool being mistaken for a sawed-off shotgun.

WAY #40: PASSIVE VOICE

This makes me grumpy…

A ruined morning routine.

You know that feeling you get when you put your socks on in the morning?

The flowers are blooming.

The birds are chirping.

The sun is shining.

All is RIGHT in the world.

You go to your kitchen (filled with giddy anticipation), reach into your cabinet & grab out a red mug for your tasty caffeinated beverage. But something is wrong - that seductive AM aroma is missing. As you pour the steamy liquid, suddenly you realize your coffee pot brewed Kool-Aid.

What a way to ruin a perfectly good morning.

You know what else makes me grumpy?

Passive voice.

Using passive voice makes your copy less engaging & less effective. It doesn't persuade readers to take action or buy into you.

Not sure how spot passive voice in your copy?

Put the phrase "by me" after each verb in your sentences. If your sentences make sense, you're using passive voice.

For example...

YIKES - You're invited (by me) to stop in and visit soon.
Makes sense? Yes...Passive voice.
YES - We invite (by me) you to stop in and visit soon.
Makes sense? No...Active voice.

YIKES - The form was processed and returned (by me).
Makes sense? Yes...Passive voice.
YES - We completed (by me) your request and mailed the form to you.
Makes sense? No...Active voice.

YIKES - A new, plain language directive was signed in the communication's office (by me).
Makes sense? Yes...Passive voice.
YES - The Communication's Director signed (by me) the new, plain language directive.
Makes sense? No...Active voice.

Eliminate passive voice from your copy & entice readers to take action. Unlike Kool-Aid in your coffee pot. Which isn't enticing at all.

WAY #41: LACK OF (TIME) CONSISTENCY

This makes me grumpy…

That time I was visiting my grandma…

In the nursing home…

And a staff member thought I lived there.

It was dark (and raining).

I was waiting for my assistant to pull my van around and pick me up.

A nurse came up to me…

Demanded to know what I was doing…

And why I wasn't in my room.

As she reached for my joystick to move me, I jerked my wheelchair away from her.

And said…

"I don't know who you think you are. But I don't live here."

Her face became a fiery flushed color, and she apologized.

I asked her if that meant I couldn't have any more red jello.

She just walked away.

You know what else makes me grumpy?

Time.

The right way to express time in copywriting is controversial.

Some write AM & PM

Others write A.M. & P.M.

Still others write am & pm.

None of those are technically wrong…

Because it's a style choice.

But the most effective way to express time in copywriting is…

a.m. & p.m.

It's effective because most of the published style guides agree about its use.

Therefore, it's the most commonly used.

This means your readers are used to seeing time expressed that way.

Express time in your copy any way you want.

But remember…be CONSISTENT.

Your readers prefer consistency above anything else.

Just make sure you put a space between the number and a.m. (or) p.m.

Otherwise, your text runs together and can create confusion for your readers.

For example…

YIKES - The customer wanted to talk about their copywriting problems at <u>9P.M</u>.

YES - The customer wanted to talk about their copywriting problems at <u>9:00 p.m</u>.

YIKES - Sally had to give her presentation at 8:00AM.

YES - Sally had to give her presentation at 8:00 a.m.

YIKES - 11pm is too late for me to edit effectively.
YES - 11:00 p.m. is too late for me to edit effectively.

Be consistent with time in your copy. It's easier than annoying a nurse.

WAY #42: THE EM DASH

This makes me grumpy…

I was waiting in line to cash out at my local Agway.

And 2 women were whisper-arguing.

I couldn't understand what they were saying. But I knew they were talking about me because they kept looking in my direction.

Finally, they approached, and one asked what I liked to be called…

Handicap…

Physically challenged…

Or disabled…

I smiled and said, "Autumn is fine. Thank you".

You know what baffles & offends your readers?

The em dash.

The em dash is the longest of all the dash marks.

You create it by pressing CTRL+ALT+minus (for MS Word) or ALT+0151 (for email) on your keyboard.

2 hyphens are often substituted for an em dash. Which is a crime in copywriting.

The em dash's purpose is to interrupt a clause—like so—to impart additional information on your readers.

But this punctuation is clunky (like cheap fashion jewelry).

It clutters up your copy & slows your readers' down.

Cut the em dash and replace with parentheses to add clarity to your copy.

Using parentheses (instead of the em dash) makes your readers' feel like you're letting them in on a secret.

For example...

YIKES - Register for the SEO training class before it fills up—faster than a hybrid car.
YES - Register for the SEO training class before it fills up (faster than a hybrid car).

YIKES - I talked to Ben—my super savvy graphic designer—about creating images for my new website.
YES - I talked to Ben (my super savvy graphic designer) about creating images for my new website.

YIKES - Upon discovering the errors—all 57 of them—my editor saved me from insurmountable embarrassment.
YES - Upon discovering the errors (all 57 of them), my editor saved me from insurmountable embarrassment.

Eliminate the em dash and replace with parentheses to add clarity to your copy. Unlike 2 women whisper-arguing about your preferred terminology.

WAY #43: LACK OF THE EN DASH

This makes me grumpy…

That time I got stuck and couldn't sit up, so I jerked my wheelchair back & forth…fast. I thought the rocking motion would force me to sit up. But instead, I fell out of my wheelchair.

That's the day I decided I wasn't Stephen Hawking. And physics wasn't my friend.

You know what else makes me grumpy?

The en dash.

The en dash is half the size of the em dash.

You create it by pressing CTRL+minus (for MS Word) or ALT+0150 (for email) on your keyboard.

The en dash is used to highlight…

Date ranges (Jan–Feb 2017)

Descriptions of distance (the Delaware–New York train)

Or amounts ($39–$79/200–300)

But oftentimes people substitute the word "to" for the en dash.

This adds unnecessary words to your copy and slows your readers' down.

Because your readers are trained to say the word "to" when they see the en dash.

Cut the word "to" from your copy and replace with the en dash to keep your readers reading steadily.

For example…

YIKES - My website training class runs August 31st to October 31st.
YES - My website training class runs August 31st–October 31st.

YIKES - I rode the Brooklyn to Hoboken bus to get to the copywriter's conference.
YES - I rode the Brooklyn–Hoboken bus to get to the copywriter's conference.

YIKES - The SEO training class costs $199 to $499 per person.
YES - The SEO training class costs $199–$499 per person.

YIKES - XYZ Marketing was in business from 2012 to 2017.
YES - XYZ Marketing was in business from 2012–2017.

YIKES - The train to Massachusetts had 15 to 20 people riding on it.
YES - The train to Massachusetts had 15–20 people riding on it.

Use the en dash to keep your readers reading steadily. Unlike physics. Which causes you to fall out of your wheelchair.

WAY #44: VALLEY GIRL WORDS

This makes me grumpy...

When I read these words:

- Really
- Whatever
- Very

Do I have big, 80s hair or spend 99.9% of my day at the mall?

No...

You know what else makes me grumpy?

Valley Girl Words. These words intensify other words without adding any real meaning. Like a Valley Girl hyped up on caffeine.

For example ...

YIKES - Steven was *really* ugly.
YES - Steven was hideous.

YIKES - Stephanie was tall or *whatever*.
YES - Stephanie was long-legged.

YIKES - Scott was *very* annoying.
YES - Scott was obnoxious.

When you AVOID Valley Girl words, you keep your copy clear and concise. Unlike a Valley Girl, who has the same personality as her 4 best friends.

WAY #45: WHEN YOU USE THE PHRASE "THE MOST___"

This makes me grumpy…

Going to my 27th job fair within one year.

Instead of going booth-to-booth filling out applications, I tested out pick-up lines.

"Let's burn some rubber together" landed me a job interview after I unintentionally hit on a hiring manager.

You know what else makes me grumpy?

When you use the phrase "the most" ____.

"The most *important*", "the most *beautiful*", "the most *whatever*".

This phrase adds unnecessary length to your copy. And makes your copy less specific.

For example…

YIKES - Breakfast is the most important meal of the day.
YES - Breakfast is a crucial meal that helps you start your day.

YIKES - I create the most beautiful logos ever.
YES - I create alluring logos that capture your personality.

YIKES - That's the most fundamental service I can offer you.
YES - That's an essential service for your success that I can offer you.

Cut the phrase "the most ___" to make your copy more concise. Unlike testing pick-up lines at a job fair.

WAY #46: LACK OF PUNS

This makes me grumpy…

That time I traveled to New York City and my wheelchair actually went through the metal detector at Port Authority.

As I squeezed through, I told the cop that I hoped the titanium rods in my back wouldn't set off the alarm because I wasn't mentally prepared to be strip searched.

He didn't react. But the person behind me spit coffee out of their mouth.

You know what else makes me grumpy?

Lack of puns in your copy.

A pun is a play on words. And it's the simplest way to add humor to your copy. So you seem personable. Show off your personality and make me laugh.

For example…

YIKES - Subscribe to The Cactus of the Month Club. Your friends will <u>be jealous.</u>
YES - Subscribe to The Cactus of the Month Club. Your friends will <u>think you're sharp.</u>

YIKES - Rent your coin-sorting machine from us. It's a <u>good</u> decision.
YES - Rent your coin-sorting machine from us. It's a <u>cents-ible</u> decision.

YIKES - Selling extra eggs from your pet chickens is a <u>great</u> idea.
YES - Selling extra eggs from your pet chickens is an <u>eggs-ellent</u> idea.

Use puns to show off your personality. Just like the possibility of an impromptu strip search by a handsome cop.

WAY #47: LACK OF STRIKETHROUGHS

This makes me grumpy...

When a stranger at the dog park tells me the weather is too warm.

Yes, I know it's hot outside. Yes, I know you're sweating. Yes, I know the humidity is oppressive. Thank you, Captain Obvious. But I can't help the dog park is half concrete. If you're so miserable, why don't you go stand over there in the poop-filled grass where it's cooler?

You know what else makes me grumpy?

Lack of strikethroughs in your copy.

A strikethrough is used to indicate a word should be removed. But instead of removing the word, leave it. It adds a little bit of humor to your copy without distracting the reader.

For example...

YIKES - When you accept my proposal, I'll send you a custom intake questionnaire.
YES - When you accept my ~~proposition~~ proposal, I'll send you a custom intake questionnaire.

YIKES - Here's my dream journal. Now you know my secrets.
YES - Here's my dream journal. Now you know ~~all~~ most of my secrets.

YIKES - My client was terrible to talk to.

YES - My client was a ~~conversational nightmare~~ delight to talk to.

Strikethroughs make me want to read more of your copy. A lot more. Unlike a Captain Obvious conversation at the dog park...which makes me want to know less. Much less.

WAY #48: UNNECESSARY USE OF "THAT"

This makes me grumpy...

That time I was in college, sleeping in my standard issue dorm room bed, and someone flopped on top of me. If I could've jumped out of bed in sheer terror, I would've.

But I just laid there...STUNNED.

I finally mustered up the courage to touch the person and felt fuzzy knee length socks. Right next to my face. And that's when I realized it was my roommate & she was blackout drunk.

As soon as she got her off my bed, she vomited all over my floor.

I'm not sure what pissed me off more...

Cleaning up whiskey-scented puke OR not getting a picture of her laying on top of me for blackmail.

You know what else makes me grumpy?

Using the word "that" in your copy.

Sometimes this word is necessary for clarity. But usually, it's followed by an additional-information phrase. It makes your copy less concise and less descriptive.

For example...

YIKES - Our office is located in a tall building <u>that is made of brick</u>.

YES - Our office is located in a <u>tall, brick building.</u>

YIKES - The book <u>that you</u> need is on my shelf.
YES - The book <u>you</u> need is on my shelf.

YIKES - The car <u>that is candy-apple red</u> goes fast.
YES - The <u>candy-apple red</u> car goes fast.

Get rid of the word "that" to keep your copy concise. Unlike your drunk roommate. Who should've cleaned her own vomit.

WAY #49: LACK OF COMMITMENT TO CURSING - PSEUDO CURSE WORDS

This makes me grumpy…

Pseudo curse words are as useful to me as Hallmark Channel Christmas Movies.

Because only in one of these delusions of grandeur can a beautiful blonde-haired girl…

Take a carriage ride from a strange, old man…

And not end up murdered.

You know what else makes me grumpy?

Not committing to cursing in your copy.

While swearing in your copy is risky, there are benefits to it. Committing to curse words like "fuck", "shit" & "damn" implies certain qualities about you…

- Independence
- Authenticity
- Confidence

It conveys a covert sense of prestige.

Swearing also…

- Promotes group solidarity.
- Strengthens group bonds.
- And excludes, or even better, includes members.

But pseudo curse words like "sh*t", "a$$" & "dang" have the opposite effect. They instantly turn readers' off. Your covert sense of prestige is blown. Readers' know you're not embracing your badassness (A.K.A your inner Beyonce).

For example...

YIKES - Don't be a <u>f@#*ing</u> sheep. Buy our kit & stand out today.
YES - Don't be a <u>fucking</u> sheep. Buy our kit & stand out today.

YIKES - Avoid exclamation marks like the <u>mofo-ing</u> plague.
YES - Avoid exclamation marks like the <u>motherfucking</u> plague.

YIKES - Register your <u>kicka$$</u> domain today for only $4.99 per month.
YES - Register your <u>kickass</u> domain today for only $4.99 per month.

Commit to using swear words in your copy to connect with readers. Which is more realistic than a Hallmark Channel Christmas Movie.

BONUS SECTION

COMMAS

USE #1 - Unite 2 Sentences with "and", "but", "or", "so"

For example...

Your website designer asked for inspiration, and you sent her cat videos.

You responded to a client email, but sent it to your mother instead.

You asked for help with commas, so here it is.

USE #2 - Separate Items in a List

For example...

I like reading tabloid magazines because the headlines are daring, short, and punny.

Accountants keep track of payroll, disbursements, and your shoe habit.

Businesses succeed because of hard work, determination, and supernatural forces.

USE #3 - Between 2 Adjectives

For example...

Everyone loves my red, maple-leaf shaped tattoos.

Nobody likes my dad's sour, smelly asparagus soup.

I don't understand why clunky, flexless boots are so popular.

USE #4 - Separate Opposite Ideas

For example…

I like friendly dogs, not snobby cats.

My logo is a caricature, not realistic.

My personality is grumpy, not bitchy.

USE #5 - Separate a Statement from a Question

For example…

You're having fun reading these examples, aren't you?

They're pretty good, aren't they?

Let's have more, shall we?

USE #6 - Format a Date

For example…

National Lumpy Rug Day is May 3, 2018. Lumpy rugs give me whiplash.

National Fight Procrastination Day is September 6, 2018. I celebrate a day late.

National Chocolate Covered Anything is Day December 16, 2018. Just say no to the grasshoppers.

USE #7 - Format a Location

For example…

My hospital of choice is in Danville, Pennsylvania. It's like Cheers—everyone knows my name.

I've never been to Disney in Bay Lake, Florida because I never want to be surrounded by giant mice.

The dog park is in Conklin, New York. Go to the people park if you want to socialize.

USE #8 - Before or After Quotations

For example…

Jennifer declared, "Autumn must be crazy for the comma."

"No, Autumn's salty about the semicolon," Steve exclaimed.

"At least she takes a stand about punctuation," April mumbled.

USE #9 - Before, After, or Around the Name of a Person

For example…

I told you that commas can be fun when you know the rules, Lucy.

Steve, your blog posts are welcomed distractions from scheduling Facebook posts.

Pizza should never have stinky anchovies on it, Amber.

USE #10 - Sentences that answer the Question "how", "when", "where", or "why"

For example…

Because I love you, I will overlook emojis in your emails.

When I snuck up on Ginger, she jumped to her paws.

Wherever you use this comma, I'll x it out with a red pen.

USE #11 - Long Phrases that Begin with "during", "from", "after"

For example…

During a football game, I embrace superstitions like sitting in the same spot and wearing the same socks.

From the time the game starts until it ends, don't talk to me.

After the football game is over, I often find myself playing couch coach and recounting the ways my team could've won.

USE #12 - Phrases that Begin with the Word "To"

For example…

To be a great editor, I need head-banging music and caffeine.

To write clear copy, you should avoid alcohol and this comma.

To accomplish the unimaginable, you need lady balls and gummy candy.

USE #13 - When Related Events Happen at the Same Time

For example…

When you hug me, I gag from the smell of your Victoria's Secret perfume.

While I make my morning coffee, I add more milk and vanilla syrup than espresso.

As soon as I see you, I duck behind an aisle to avoid you.

USE #14 - Before or Around Words like "nevertheless", "however", or "yes", etc.

For example…

Nevertheless, you noticed me and said hello.

I said hi, however, I couldn't remember your name.

Yes, I know avoiding you was rude but so is not remembering your name.

USE #15 To Set Off a Thought that Interrupts Sentence Flow

For example…

I, The Grumpy Grammarian, demand you stop drinking decaf.

My ideal pizza, like the Ninja Turtles, always has extra cheese on it.

Your grandma, who loves you an awful lot, got 13 of her friends to buy your product.

SEMICOLONS

USE #1 - Separate Two Complete Sentences that are Closely Related

For example...

You used a paper plate as a rainbownet; your hair held its fabulous shape.

Punctuation doesn't have to be boring; look at how much fun you're having.

Your business partner liked the new about page because it had only 3 commas; I'm just that good.

Notice that each phrase, before and after the semicolon, is a complete sentence. But the second sentence must clarify or expand upon the first sentence.

USE #2 - To Replace a Comma When You Need to Clarify Items in a List

For example...

I accomplished 3 items on my to-do list: showering, because BO should be taken seriously; meeting with a client, so I could make their words magical; and showering again, because sometimes public places gross me out.

Notice that if you replaced the semicolons with commas, you'd have a confused mess.

COLONS

USE #1 - Introduce a List

For example...

You have 3 choices in life: latte, cappuccino, or macchiato.

Copywriting has 3 rules: be clear, be compelling, and be concise.

My wheelchair has only been 3 colors: matte black, glossy black, and pastel black.

Notice that the words following the colon do NOT form a complete sentence. So you couldn't use semicolons.

USE #2 To Answer a Question or Complete a Thought

For example...

Autumn has just one question: what's your favorite punctuation?

You got what you worked for: the sexiest little black dress and a matching car were your reward.

Enquiring minds want to know one thing: are you drunk with punctuation power?

Notice that the words following the colon DO form a complete sentence. So you could use a period instead of a colon.

FINAL NOTES ON SEMICOLONS & COLONS

When I'm copy editing for my clients, I remove ALL semicolons & colons.

Because as you remember, copywriting has 3 rules…

To be clear. To be compelling. And to be concise.

So save semicolons & colons for novels or memoirs or (if you're old school) emojis.

Outro

We're at the point where I'm supposed to say "goodbye" to you.

I can't bring myself to end this book, and the conversation about copy editing. I've never been good at ending anything…

A TV series (because spin-offs).

My relationship with sugar or coffee (lattes are the best of both worlds).

A joke without laughing while I'm telling it.

But I know conclusions are necessary. And, truth be told, I like an ending that's wrapped in a tidy bow. Neat like my whiskey.

Unfortunately, this isn't the case. And I'm not one of *those* writers.

If I could, I'd have some famous writer compose a proper conclusion for this book. But all the good ones are dead, and Stephen King doesn't like nonfiction.

Now, we're at an impasse. And I don't have any one-liners left. So keep up the good copy edits and think of me fondly every time you encounter an awkward situation.

#WWTGGD (What Would The Grumpy Grammarian Do?)

Made in the USA
San Bernardino, CA
05 May 2019